SUSPEND YOUR DISBELIEF

...and other short stories that are long on wisdom

Aaron Montgomery

For my wife Nimisha and our daughter Diya,
who inspire me to be the best I can
possibly be each and every day.

———

In loving memory of Uncle Johnny
1938–2020

TABLE OF CONTENTS

ACKNOWLEDGMENTS

To my wife, Nimisha Parikh, who has supported
this project from the front, back, and side—a loving
coach, fan, partner, and critic, often in the same day

To my mother, Debra Montgomery, who has patiently
always indulged ambition and allowed me to believe
I could do whatever I wanted in life right up until I did

To my friends Will Alston and Mac Grayson, who
encouraged me to share more stories more often

To my friend, Marcus Hodges, who sees my potential
and holds me accountable for reaching it

To my friend, Andy Stefanovich,
who made me rethink my limits

To my coach, Nhat Pham, who helped me take the
next step, and the next one, and the next one

To my guide, Avery Roth, who helped me grow
my faith rather than shrink my goals

To Laila Weir for helping me fine-tune my voice

To Julie Karen Hodgins for helping me
get the "look and feel" just right

To Quincy Sutton, Khalid Birdsong, John Mating, and
Paul Westover for adding texture through their art

To all my family, friends, and supporters, everyone
who was willing to support me in any way at any
time, I appreciate you all and love you very much

INTRODUCTION

A ll these years later, I still remember the exact moment I got hooked. I was about seven years old, it was a rainy Saturday, and my mother gave me a book of Aesop's Fables to help me pass the time stuck indoors. At the time, I had no concept of Aesop's historical significance, or of the significance of fable traditions in general. All I knew was that I couldn't put the book down.

Each new story was better than the last, and before I even realized it, I'd devoured the entire book. Literally, hundreds of fables that were meant to entertain me through the whole dreary weekend, done in a matter of hours. I begged my mother to drive me to the library to find some more, hoping beyond hope that the book, entitled "The Complete Collection of Aesop's Fables," had maybe left a few for the director's cut.

It hadn't, so I spent the rainy Sunday afternoon combing the library stacks, learning about other fable traditions. I was especially drawn to West African folktales and the "Old Plantation" folklore inspired by them.

I loved the stories. The simple structure, the relatable characters, the anthropomorphic animals... but more than anything, I loved the moral at the end of the story. The neat, tidy lesson that summarized the point of the anecdote and made it simultaneously more memorable and applicable. Those clever aphorisms were almost a type of mnemonic device to ensure you'd remember the deep, powerful truths long after the details of the story grew hazy. And, in the best cases, they ensured the story never grew hazy at all.

My attraction to aphorisms was deepened by my grandparents, who loved what they called "wisdom sayings." Devout Christians who read the Bible daily, they were particularly drawn to the Books of Ecclesiastes and Book of Proverbs, collections of ancient Jewish wisdom that were said to be handed down from King Solomon the Wise. I still remember my grandfather quoting his favorite scriptures, as well as his own expressions inspired by them, and can just as easily recall them now as when I last heard them many years ago.

It is no wonder then that now, almost 35 years later, I find that I'm most comfortable relating knowledge and experience through stories and their morals. As Paw Paw would have said, "You're only good at what you practice," and I've been practicing a very specific sort of storytelling for most of my life.

I wrote this book to share some of those stories, and the lessons they contain, with you. But more importantly, I want to encourage you to capture and share your own. As you read them, please remember that these stories are about me—not because they are the best stories I know, but because they are the stories that I know best. I'm not the hero; I'm just a character, like Anansi the spider or Br'er Fox. The hero is the lesson.

I hope that by sharing these stories I'll convince you that all knowledge is knowledge worth sharing, and that every experience is an opportunity to grow, learn, and share. But, to really hear them, you have to suspend your disbelief.

Thank you for reading.

SUSPEND YOUR DISBELIEF

Our high school's production of *Into the Woods* was amazing. We had a great story, a stellar cast, and direction from some of the most talented and caring drama teachers in our area.

It was a once-in-a-lifetime experience. We performed to a sold-out theater every night and drew some national attention, collecting several accolades along the way—including an invitation to the National Thespian Festival.

My high school had more than its fair share of theater talent over the years, but this was the first time the school had ever earned a spot in the festival. What's more, we were to perform on the main stage, a distinction that was reserved for the best of the best.

We were just a small private school from the midwest, but the other schools were on a whole other level. They hailed from places like New York, Los Angeles, and Las Vegas, where school plays are not just an after-school activity, but a pipeline to the mainstream entertainment industry. One look at their sets, makeup, and costumes, and you felt like you were on Broadway and not at a high school exhibition.

Our club, on the other hand, was a bit ... *scrappier*. Our costumes were homemade and often cobbled together with remnants from prior shows. We did our own makeup (and over time got pretty skilled at it). And our set! Our set was a literal embodiment of the concept of the willing suspension of disbelief.

As *Into the Woods* takes place, well, in the woods, we needed lots of trees. Our solution was to purchase giant cardboard tubes, at least eight feet tall and several inches in diameter. A few weeks before we opened production, we came in on a weekend, rolled them all in, textured them with papier-mâché, and painted them brown. Then we added leaves, birds, and other accents freehand to create our own enchanted forest.

When we finished, I loved our set. It was a testament to that scrappiness of ours, our creativity, and frankly our ingenuity in finding such a simple, yet elegant, solution. But when we took in the other teams' sets, there was no comparison. One play took place on a boat, and the set was like watching *Titanic*. Another that took place on an island had a set like an afternoon on the beach. And I've seen television sets less detailed than that for a third play set in an apartment.

Seeing these professional-quality sets night after night, as our main performance approached, completely sapped our confidence. Our once-enchanted forest turned back into a bunch of cardboard tubes. It was past midnight, and time for Cinderella to go home.

During the morning run-through, our teacher, Dr. Moss, could feel the lag in energy. Reading a room and being sensitive to others' moods was one of his strengths. Rather than ask us if we were OK, he came at the problem indirectly and delivered a passionate speech about the actor's role in creating the suspension of disbelief.

> *Theater works because of the partnership between the actors and the audience. The actors commit to their characters and the story, and the audience commits to going on a journey with those actors. The audience at Stratford knew the witches in MacBeth weren't actual witches. Our audience knows this isn't an actual forest. But for the 90 minutes or so that we perform, our job is to convince them to believe, and reward that belief with an incredible journey.*

We did commit, our audience came along with us, and we gave our best performance ever. It was flawless, we left everything we had to give on that stage, we got a standing ovation, and we all learned a very valuable lesson that day.

The concept of the willing suspension of disbelief is primarily an artistic idea, but I've found it to be a useful illustration for helping people break out of their cognitive constraints and remove barriers to problem-solving.

When you're facing a tough problem, sometimes the problem is all you can see. The constraints are there, and they're very real, but so is your imagination. And often, using it to simply suspend your disbelief and imagine a world without constraints can be a powerful first step towards a solution. In fact, in many cases it can be the only step you really need.

No problem is truly unsolvable. Even if the only solutions seem theoretical, it's worth considering them just to ignite your brain. Remember that at one time, being able to fly was impossible, but not 60 years after the Wright Brothers figured it out, there were human beings on the moon.

Whatever solutions exist in the world begin first in the imagination, and the imagination is most powerful when we let it run freely. ■

"You weren't supposed to see this."

YOU CAN DO IT RIGHT, OR YOU CAN DO IT TWICE

When I was 11 years old, my mother decided to repaint our house. Since I was practically an adult (at least in my own eyes), she told me I could choose whatever color I wanted for my room, so long as I painted it myself. I saw this as an awesome deal: I could finally personalize my room—and getting to paint it myself was a bonus!

Though I'd never painted an entire room myself, I loved to paint. The actual painting part, that is. I abhorred the other parts of the job: laying down dropcloth, priming the walls, taping the corners and edges, sanding down rough spots. So, viewing these steps as suggestions more than requirements, I skipped them.

It went about as you'd expect, and by the time I was finished, the room looked like a toddler's coloring book—a very expensive, not-so-fun coloring book. I'd cut corners in an effort to make the job faster, easier, and a little less painful. In the end, all I got was a bad paint job...and a valuable lesson.

The admonition to do it right or do it twice isn't just a caution against laziness and carelessness. Often, well-intended, hard-working, judicious people can make the same mistake. When I started my last company, my partners and I were *ridiculously* cost-conscious. We had taken investor money to build a new concept, and we were determined not to waste a cent on anything frivolous or unnecessary. Every expenditure went through rigorous *"do we really need that?"* analysis.

For the most part, I don't regret that approach. Frugality is a virtue that more entrepreneurs should practice. But, at the same time, you can take it too far. And we did, by underinvesting in some key areas of our business where we most needed a solid ROI. We cheaped out on everything—our website, our retail presence, even our staffing model—and, as a result, we had a number of false starts before eventually finding our rhythm. Worst of all, buying the cheap version before we ended up buying the more expensive one anyway just made the expen-

sive option *even more expensive*—meaning, of course, that we burned cash even faster.

So, as my 11-year-old self would tell you: Don't cut corners. Seek expert opinions where necessary, and then do it right. ∎

INSIGHTS

IF YOU CAN TOUCH IT, YOU CAN CATCH IT

Gary Hills was a tough coach, but also a compassionate one. He gave everything to his players and expected our 100 percent effort in return.

I had just enough natural athleticism to excel at football, but I lacked fundamentals. I'd picked up the sport as a high school sophomore—much later than most of my peers. My teammates on our high school team were veritable veterans compared to me, some having played for a decade.

Notwithstanding the hundreds of games I'd watched on television, and the thousands of hours of backyard catch I'd played, I really didn't have a feel for the basics. Still, I picked up most of the skills pretty quickly in pre-season training— blocking, tackling, even properly receiving a handoff, which I hadn't even realized was a thing.

But the hardest skill to get down was catching. Sure, I could play a game of catch and toss the ball around, but hauling in 60-yard throws over my shoulder in full stride was a whole different game. After one particularly bad drop that frustrated my QB and teammates, Coach finally pulled me aside:

"Montgomery, what happened on that one?"

"It was a little ahead of me, Coach."

"But you touched it."

"I know. Just barely, though."

"Well, if you can touch it, you can catch it. So, don't worry about catching it, just touch it … and then reel it in."

That brief exchange radically shifted my mindset. Being a "receiver" might sound passive—almost like I just had to run somewhere and wait for the ball—but in reality my end of the bargain was to do *everything I possibly could* to catch the ball.

If that meant picking up a little speed at the end of a route, or cutting off a little early, or extending for a jump ball on a high throw, that was all part of the job. Anything that was "catchable" not only *could* be caught, but *should* be caught.

That extra effort was what it was all about.

So remember: You can catch anything you can touch. Always try to find your agency in any given situation. If something is within your reach, even if only barely, then you can conceivably reel it in. Whether that's a goal, a new opportunity, a promotion, or whatever, don't quit on your route and don't wait for the perfect pass—put yourself in a position to catch and reel that sucker in! ■

HARD WORK BEATS TALENT WHEN TALENT DOESN'T WORK HARD

Academically speaking, I was what you'd call a late bloomer. My grades weren't very good, classes were a chore, and parent-teacher conferences went nuclear so often that I could essentially plan my groundings well in advance. The worst part was that they always seemed to end with the same comment: "Aaron is a bright kid, and he'd do well if he only tried harder."

Now, teachers could have been saying that to spare my mom's feelings. But once I heard it enough times … around about the middle of seventh grade … I realized there really were only two possibilities. Either a) I was pretty smart and needed to figure out how to put in the effort, or b) I actually wasn't that smart and would have to work harder to compensate.

I figured I could test the question by putting in some effort and seeing what happened. But I really didn't know how to start. After so many years of avoiding hard work, I didn't really even know what it looked like. So I went to the brightest guy I knew, my best friend Reuben. Everything seemed to come easily for him. He had the best grades, the highest test scores, and the teachers all loved him.

I really admired his intelligence and I told him so, practically begging him to take me on as a project and tutor me. To my surprise, he was clearly taken aback. He asked, "What do you mean? How would I tutor you?"

"I thought you could teach me what you know."

"I don't know this stuff. I just study."

"How do you study?"

I swear, I didn't even know what he meant. I had no idea what studying was. I thought that was what we were doing in school all day. When Reuben saw my look of utter bafflement, he finally understood what he was up against. He was going to have to be my "Yoda" and start all the way from the beginning.

The thing is, Reuben really didn't think of himself as a "smart kid" at all. In his mind, he was just following a system. He'd learn a new concept through practice and drill until he understood it intuitively. Sometimes he got it right away; sometimes it took a while. But that process was his only key to success.

Now, Reuben was, and is, *very* smart. But when he laid it out for me like this, suddenly it just clicked. Reuben had the best grades in our class—and he'd just showed me the recipe. Coming from the bottom, which is where I was, I knew it was going to be a long way up. But, even if his "secret" made me half as successful as he was, it would still be quite a turnaround.

I learned to speed-read, take notes, and use flashcards. I attended extra-credit sessions and joined study groups. I did my homework and reviewed the answers with my teacher. It sounds so basic, but until that point I'd just gone to class and gone home expecting to have learned everything by absorption.

After almost 12 months of learning and mastering Reuben's techniques, I turned my mostly C and D averages into a respectable 3.0 GPA in eighth grade. Reuben, our valedictorian, had a 4.0. I decided to make *that* my goal for high school.

And I did it. I carried a 4.0 average throughout all four years of high school and learned to integrate sports, theater, choir, and a host of community service activities. I was accepted to nine colleges, including Harvard, Princeton, Dartmouth, and UPenn, and most offered me full rides.

When I tell my story now, people assume that my academic success was a result of my talent or intelligence. But that can't be it, because I wasn't inherently more talented on the day I graduated with honors from Harvard than I was when I got grounded for failing seventh-grade science. I'd just learned to work harder.

Of course, hard work and talent don't have to be diametrically opposed, but sadly they often are. Maybe extra-talented people too easily get used to being able to slide by and never learn to pull themselves up with brute effort. And that's too bad: Hard work alone is a great equalizer, but married with talent it can make someone virtually unstoppable.

Even now, when I meet candidates, if given a choice between talent and work ethic, I choose effort 10 times out of 10—unless of course that person's talent *is* putting in a ton of effort! ■

Well, Aaron has been giving 100% effort since our last conference, but the problem is it's 10% on Monday, 22% on Tuesday…

FAILURE PREPARES FOR SUCCESS, BUT SUCCESS WON'T PREPARE FOR FAILURE

A few days after arriving on campus for my first year of college, I was invited to a "mixer" where I could get to know some of my classmates. To help get things going, we played a Bingo-style ice breaker game, with each square being a piece of biographical information that might apply to someone in the room.

The object was to cover the squares by meeting people, learning about them, and seeing if any of the squares applied to them. The first person who had interviewed enough people to cover all their squares won the game.

Most squares were softballs, truly designed to get some conversation going between a bunch of homesick teenagers. Things like "grew up on a farm" or "born outside the US." Some probed a bit more, like "plays saxophone" or "first to go to college."

About an hour in, everyone's boards were mostly filled and the game had clearly had its desired effect. People were learning about each other and having a great time doing it. And that's when I noticed that more than a dozen people were waiting to talk to me!

One of the people in line spoke up:

"Excuse me, I heard you failed a test before?"

"Yeah, lots of times," I replied. "I'm not the only one here, am I?"

"Uh, yeah, you are."

I was stunned. Out of this crowd of freshmen, no one had ever failed. I addressed the larger group, and it was confirmed—not a single soul in that room had ever gotten lower than a C. I was surprised, but not the least bit embarrassed. If anything, it felt good to be someone who had overcome challenges and made it to Harvard, rather than a person who felt somehow predestined to be there.

I was a late bloomer in school, and my mother wisely and patiently instilled a sense of pride in taking the hard route towards something that others found easy. I had failed before, and I expected that I would again. It carried no sting or stigma for me, because I had already learned that you can fail and live to tell the tale.

I signed those Bingo boards like they were autographs after a ball game, sharing stories about my failures to the group of astonished first years. Over the coming months, many of them got their first failing grades ever as they adjusted

"I'll tell you how I got here—hours and hours of hard visualization."

to the challenges and rigors of college versus the familiar comfort of high school. I was able to support and encourage them, boosted by the credibility of my experience and the fact that despite my challenges I was right there with them. I shared that my failures were what propelled me and that theirs could propel them.

If you look at any number of successful people, whether in sports, arts, business, or politics, you'll find that they were forged by their failures. And, typically, the sooner you fail at something and learn the lessons that come with it, the better.

Everyone takes an "L" sometimes. But, while L can stand for "Loss," remember this: It can also stand for "Learn." ∎

THEY'RE
ALL GOOD,
UNTIL
THEY AREN'T

Mr. James was my first barber. My uncle brought me to see him because he was *his* first barber, too. All in all, he'd worked at the same shop, from the same chair, for more than 50 years.

That steadiness was evident in his consistent work. You didn't go to him for the trendiest, latest style—he wasn't a chef, but he was a damn good cook. In fact, I used to say "you don't go to Mr. James for the fancy steak, but you'll get a really good hamburger every single time."

In the 15 years I saw him, he must have cut my hair nearly a thousand times, and I can't remember a single bad cut. So it's fair to say that I got a little bit spoiled.

Then I went away to college, meaning I would need to find a new barber. We didn't have Yelp or Google in those days, so my inquiries were limited to asking around or interrogating people with particularly nice haircuts. After a bit, I found one who came highly recommended.

Fritz seemed like a great find. He minded all the details; he was careful, thorough, and willing to take his time to get it just right. When he showed me the mirror, his work was *amazing*. Every line, every corner, every single hair perfectly coiffed and cleaned.

Eager to replace Mr. James, I made a standing weekly appointment with Fritz but, after a couple months, I noticed his meticulous work began to fall off. He started coming in later and later, and his customer service plummeted. But, worst of all, the cuts themselves, which had once been so meticulous and careful, got so sloppy and careless that I found myself looking for a new barber all over again.

Fritz taught me a valuable lesson about the difference between auditioning well and performing well. Sure, you may move ahead with the hope that things will work out long-term, but you should also acknowledge the fact that they rarely do. My relationship with Mr. James was forged over generations. He was *my* barber. Fritz helped me out in a pinch. He was *a* barber.

Not every date will end in marriage, but most marriages started with a single date. Be cautiously optimistic with every new encounter, hoping for the best, but preparing for something less. ∎

INSIGHTS

IF YOU PINCH A BUBBLE TOO HARD, IT BREAKS

Years ago, I ran the credit desk for a large industrial-supply company.

It was an incredible opportunity. The company had a remarkable track record for developing young management talent, and part of their "secret sauce" was to throw you right in the water and let you try to swim.

There was some risk in that approach, to be sure, but it was almost all *their* risk, and the benefit was a team that learned valuable lessons quickly and could add more value more quickly than otherwise.

One example of that risk was giving me, only two years out of college, the power to place orders on a "credit hold," essentially refusing to ship orders for customers whose accounts were past due.

The company typically allowed 30-day terms on new orders. The bad debt write-offs were marginal, but some of our customers inevitably fell behind—leaving me, the credit manager, to decide whether to continue shipping while we worked out an agreement, or shut down their account and insist they pay immediately.

The decision seemed clear to me. I was evaluated on how much bad debt our branch had, and how long on average our customers took to pay. So, for me, the rule for late payers was clear: You don't pay, you don't play.

If someone fell behind on an order, I'd shut them down until they caught up. If it happened again, I'd shut them down again *and* insist they pay in advance. If it happened a third time, like if a card was ever declined, I'd tell them they should take their business somewhere else.

After about six months of my leadership and direction, the mid-year budget results were out, and my branch had the lowest bad debt write-offs, the lowest account aging, and the highest number of suspended or managed accounts. All as a direct result of my hands-on, aggressive approach.

Unfortunately, my colleagues on the sales side did not have the stellar results that I'd accomplished. Their sales had slowed, the growth rate had flattened, and new accounts were taking longer to ramp up. The results were a real head-scratcher for everyone. Everyone that is, except for our branch manager. For him, the numbers told a clear story that he'd seen a hundred times before. I had pinched the bubble so hard that it broke.

If you've ever blown bubbles as a kid, you know that you can pinch them a little and the air will move to one side or the other. But if you pinch too hard—and there's a very, very fine line—the bubble pops. If I'd pinched only a little less, maybe I could have slowed the credit losses at only a slight cost to sales. Instead, my scorched-earth policy left us in a hole that would take time to emerge from.

This is the challenge of teamwork, in a nutshell. We work together, but our work is the sum of our individual contributions. What's good for me isn't always good for you and vice versa. But the goal is to figure out what's best for us all. That takes patience, and practice, but it's worth it if it helps avoid a bunch of broken bubbles. ∎

CLOSED MOUTHS DON'T GET FED

A talented friend of mine recently left his job of many years. He said he was frustrated because the job lacked advancement opportunities and he'd never been chosen for any special projects—despite his tenure, reputation, and consistently solid performance.

It seemed like a major loss for the firm, as my friend was not only exceptionally skilled at the job, but he also loved the work, his teammates, and the company. Shocked that his company could whiff so badly on something like this, especially in such a competitive market, I asked him:

"How did your managers justify passing you over for all these years?"

"I guess they figured I'd stick around forever," he replied.

"But what did they say? How did they explain the logic behind choosing someone else over you?"

"They never said anything."

"But what did they say when you asked them to explain themselves?"

"What do you mean? I never asked."

Wow. He never even asked. It's hard for me to blame the company for not giving someone something they may never have known they wanted.

There are a million reasons why people don't get what they want in life. Not asking for it should never be one of them. Closed mouths don't get fed, and even the open ones don't always get as much as they want, so it's always better to have asked and been denied than never to have asked at all. ■

INSIGHTS

IF YOU CAN'T HIDE IT, FEATURE IT

When I was a kid and newspapers were still a thing, people actually shopped for homes in the classified ads.

It was a far cry from the online listings we enjoy today, with their plethora of photos and details! Back then, you mostly got a brief description written in shorthand to meet the paper's character limits. Take this actual example from 1988: "827 Grasser, 4 bd, 1.5 ba, basemt, gar, f/p, nice home $129,900."

Showings were the big reveal: You had no idea what you were going to see, what neighborhood the house was in, what condition it was in, nothing.

On top of that, real estate agents used what I'll call *creative language* to entice people to check out homes. "Handyman's dream" was basically a euphemism for "money pit," "EZ commute" meant the house was probably near a noisy highway, "cozy" meant small, "charming" meant old, and "scenic" could mean anything from large windows to a missing roof.

It worked, though, because shoppers were in on the lingo and everyone knew the game. The "game" being that, while every house had flaws, any agent worth anything was expected to sell through them and find the right buyer for that home. And one of the most effective ways to do that was to feature those very flaws, instead of trying to hide them.

No matter what a listing says, everyone who buys a house evaluates it eventually. No use trying to hide something that potential buyers will inevitably see. So, rather than apologize for their listings' shortcomings, agents highlighted those features as the houses' core benefits. It's a brilliant strategy, when you think about it. Not only does it function as a clever way to draw attention, but it also serves as a disclaimer of sorts, and a rather effective one at that.

We see this all the time today, so much that we may not even notice it. Think of all the dive bars that bear that once-negative moniker proudly. Or the budget airlines that broadcast their no-frills model, rather than disappointing travelers who might otherwise expect the five-star experience. The reality is that features and flaws are largely a matter of perspective.

Some years back, I opened a car dealership that was "under construction" for well over a year. Half the lot was covered in thick red dirt that found its way into and onto all our cars. No one wants to test-drive a dirty car, let alone buy one. How could we sell in an environment like that?

The obvious solution was to finish the construction, but that was going to take as long as it took. In the meantime, another option was to feature the dust we were asking our guests to pardon. We began giving coupons for free details and new floor mats to everyone who bought a car. We couldn't remove the dirt, but we could remove its impact by acknowledging the situation and addressing it proactively.

Hiding flaws is difficult. It's deceptive, and deception is exhausting. Rather than spending energy trying to avoid being found out, I'd rather spend mine addressing the issue head-on. That means trying to fix my flaws where I can. And where I can't, it means putting a spotlight on them and making them a part of the story. ■

DON'T GO BEHIND THE COUNTER

After finding an error on a utility bill, I phoned my provider to have it corrected. It seemed like a fairly straightforward concern, so I expected it to be a quick call.

The customer service agent was very helpful. Thoughtful, pleasant, compassionate, and thorough. Within a couple minutes, she had identified the problem and knew exactly how to resolve it. The difficulty came when she tried to explain it all to me.

I couldn't make it out. It was English, sure, but the word combinations meant nothing to me. Apparently my account was "flagged" during an "account sweep" by the "resolutions group" and scheduled for "escalation." She could resolve it by "re-coding" the account and mentioned some of the series of letters and numbers that she would "add to my profile." Frankly, I didn't really care, and I couldn't have understood it even if I did.

My ideal script would have been something more like this:

"I'm sorry, Mr. Montgomery. I see the error and will correct it and credit your account. Is there anything else I can help you with today?"

And if I asked what happened:

"Apparently, a surcharge was added to your account that shouldn't have been, so I removed it."

And if I asked how that happened:

"Your account was grouped with some other accounts in error, so I'll add a note to ensure it never happens again."

I could go on, but the point is that each statement is plain, simple, and clear. It answers the question directly without extra information.

Staying in front of the counter is an important customer service skill, especially when you work in a complicated space. You've experienced this with airlines, health care providers, mechanics, mobile phone retailers. Just knowing your stuff isn't enough. Knowing it in a way that you can communicate effectively is key.

The most challenging aspect of industry and company jargon is the insidious way it creeps up on you and becomes your own. You use these words, abbreviations, acronyms, and expressions so often that they feel like normal language to you—but they aren't.

So give yourself a periodic language audit. Re-read your emails, ask others to flag words or phrases you use that are unfamiliar to them, and discipline yourself to communicate effectively by committing to plain-speak over jargon.

Reliance on jargon and industry short-hand results in more isolation, poorer communication, less connection, and weaker problem-solving skills. Come out from behind the counter, relate to others in a more universal way, and restrict the closed-off thinking that binds us into such patterns to begin with.

We accept that we can't effectively serve customers or clients if we don't listen to them and understand them, but we need to realize that the same is true if they can't understand us. ■

I'm sorry,
but until we run
a comprehensive
diagnostic on the
firmware update
drivers, I can't
help you find
the "any" key?

THE BEST WAY TO EAT AN ELEPHANT IS ONE BITE AT A TIME

The first time I co-founded an investor-backed company, my partners and I were so excited, so energetic, so optimistic, and so … overwhelmed! We'd spent the better part of a year making pitches, editing business plans, and raising capital, only to find that the hardest work—actually building and sustaining a successful venture—still lay ahead.

The to-do list was long and seemed to grow with every meeting, every day. We still needed a website, a bank account, an office, a team! And every macro activity, like

"build website," had dozens of micro activities beneath it, like "secure domain," "find web host," and "hire designer."

The list got overwhelming, and the overwhelm led to frustration, which in turn led to procrastination, which only made the list get longer even faster. And then the cycle would repeat.

The only way out was to take the long view. We realized that what we were trying to build was a massive new thing, and that massive new things took a lot of work. The kind of work that can't all be done at once, so we shouldn't expect it to be.

The only way forward was to break the tasks up into steps and tackle them sequentially. We had to be impatient for effort but patient for results, because some things would require time to season and grow, no matter how hard we pushed or pulled. But if we followed this process consistently, eventually we'd find ourselves on the way to accomplishing a great thing.

It's like the old saying goes: There's only one way to eat an elephant, and that's one bite at a time. The analogy works so well because it's applicable to so many aspects of life. Whether it's a big project at work or school, a sizable debt, building a company, saving for retirement, or even raising a child—no matter the challenge and no matter how big— bite by bite works every time. ■

INSIGHTS

DEFENSIVE PEOPLE ARE EXPENSIVE PEOPLE

Laura was one of the more talented teammates I'd ever recruited. She was skilled, committed, learned quickly, and could catch just about anything you threw her way. Her only problem was that she was *never* wrong. At least to hear her tell it.

If you ever tried to give her any kind of feedback or constructive criticism, you were sure to be met with so many defensive explanations that you'd eventually just give up.

I hated to see her talent go to waste. Sure, she was an all-star, but if no one could help her improve, it was only a matter of time until she fell behind. After one particularly egregious example, I decided to take a different approach, and sent her this note.

Laura,

　　I've heard so many positive things about you since you joined us. So glad to hear you're off to such a quick and productive start, and I hope the experience has been all you hoped.

　　I want to offer you some advice that I think can help you. At our company, we rely on near-constant feedback and coaching to help us get better quickly and, in my opinion, it's a big part of the success we've had to date. When I overheard teammates offering you some coaching last night, you seemed pretty resistant, and I'd encourage you to really try to get past that, because it will almost certainly limit your growth in the long run.

　　To illustrate, consider two teammates:

　　We'll call the first one "Wilma"—tremendously talented, highly skilled, and basically point-and-click on day 1—a solid 8 out of 10. Her only downside is that she doesn't know what she doesn't know and, worse, she doesn't like to be shown.

The other teammate, "Betty" is maybe a solid 5. Not as talented or skilled, but since she knows that, she's hungry for feedback and often seeks it out. Every time Betty gets feedback, she listens carefully and applies it, and because of that she gets 0.5 percent better at her job every single day.

Meanwhile, Wilma doesn't get better because a) she doesn't want feedback and b) people have just given up trying to instruct her, because they don't want the hassle of arguing. She doesn't necessarily get worse, either, but look at Figure 1 to see what happens over time.

Month one Wilma dominates, month two still shows a huge gap, but note what begins to happen by the fourth month—and the fifth and sixth. Suddenly Wilma looks like a washout, a bust after only six months. And Betty is the team's new MVP.

Try to see feedback as a gift rather than a punishment. Your teammates' advice, this note, and any other feedback you get are just evidence that we all care and want you to succeed.

Laura turned the corner almost immediately, within the year she was promoted to manager, and she sent lots of notes just like this one to *her* team. ∎

*And as you can see here in Figure 1, at this rate we'll
be parting ways somewhere around month five …*

DIAGNOSE, THEN PRESCRIBE

About a year ago, I had the worst toothache ever. It hurt when I ate, drank, or even breathed, and the throbbing pain was nearly constant.

Weirdly, it had started out of nowhere and immediately went from 0 to 100. My attempt to self-diagnose with WedMD only led to more panic, so I decided that the wiser course might be to visit an actual dentist.

My dentist is one of the best in the game. Sensing my urgency, he saw me the next day, and when I arrived he wasted no time at all for his thorough examination. He asked me a litany of questions to understand my problem: "When does it hurt?" "Is it a dull ache or a sharp pain?" "Does it hurt to eat or drink?" "Does it hurt to breathe? "Can you sleep through the pain?"

And so the line of questioning went for several minutes, before he even asked me to open my mouth and say "Ahhhh."

When he finally inspected the site, it only confirmed what he'd suspected—my bite was off. Not by much, and an untrained eye wouldn't even have noticed it, but apparently even the tiniest offset can result in tremendous pain if left unattended. The best part was that all I needed to fix it was two or three seconds with a dental bur. No drugs, no surgeries, and no more pain.

A few weeks later, my wife had a similar experience, only instead of a toothache it was a pain in her eye. Constant, unbearable pain that came out of nowhere and made it difficult for her to function normally or even see. She also checked WebMD, saw the futility in it, and scheduled an appointment with *her* doctor, but that's where the similarities end.

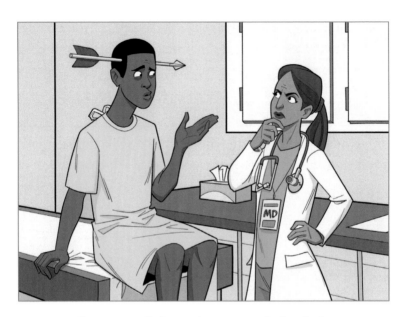

Can you recall the precise moment the headaches started? Were you doing anything unusual?

Her opthamologist didn't ask any questions beyond "what happened?" She took a hard look in the eye and, thinking she saw the offending object, quickly ordered a biopsy. She extracted the dark, spherical matter from my wife's eye and quickly sent it off to the lab to help resolve the conundrum. But her action, and haste, seemed to affirm our worst fears— cancer—a tremendously scary proposition in any case, but especially so close to the brain.

The three-day wait for the results was terrifying. When we finally got a call from the lab, it concluded that the object was an "inorganic substance" (e.g., a metal, synthetic fabric, or even table salt). The entire ordeal caused lots of worry, not to mention the several days of wasted time, doctor visits, and bills. And to add insult to injury, the pain stopped after her eye got flushed at the lab during the biopsy prep.

Most of this would have been avoided if the first doctor had been more thorough in diagnosing the issue before jumping to one of many possible conclusions about treatment. She didn't ask how long my wife had been in pain or whether she'd recently done anything that could have gotten something into her eye. She didn't ask if my wife had tried to flush her eye out. She didn't even ask if she wore contacts. If she had asked any of these things, they might have triggered my wife's recollection or at least offered alternative explanations.

Pattern recognition is human nature, and an important part of it. It makes us efficient problem solvers and allows us to use our experience to build proficiency. But sometimes it can lead to a false positive, when the pattern we think we recognize is really something else entirely.

Even if you think you know, it's always worth taking an extra moment to properly diagnose a problem before you prescribe its solution. If your first inclination was right, testing it won't cost you much. If you were wrong, it could save you a ton. ■

DON'T BUILD THE CHURCH FOR EASTER

My wife and I love to entertain, and our daughter's first birthday was as good a reason as any to throw a big party for all our friends and family.

We invited over 100 people and found an amazing, experienced caterer to provide food and drinks. She gave us tons of options and proposed a wonderful menu. But every time we looked it over, we felt like it was missing something.

She suggested we serve chicken, but we also wanted beef, so we decided to serve both. She suggested vegetarian options, but we also wanted vegan options, so we decided on both. She suggested beer and wine, but we also wanted spirits. She suggested cake, but we also wanted pie.

And on and on it went. Chocolate *and* vanilla, cream pies *and* fruit pies, reds *and* whites, imports *and* domestics … By the time we were done adding in those "missing somethings," we had food and drink for every type, taste, and preference. Our thought was that it was "better to have and not need than to need and not have."

Our caterer counseled us against this approach, warning that it would be very expensive and likely quite wasteful, but we were undeterred.

When the day arrived, our guests began arriving right on time at 2 p.m., and before we knew it our house was completely full. Yet hardly anyone went anywhere near the food! Most had already eaten lunch. We'd mentioned that we'd serve food, but no one in their right mind would have imagined this much!

As expected, the final bill for the food, drinks, desserts, and serving help was astronomical. The quality was great and

those that did eat raved about it. But the vast majority of it went untouched. What a waste.

How had I whiffed so hugely? After reflection, I realized that it was because I'd gotten caught up in trying to make *all* of the guests happy *all* of the time. In trying to plan for every possible wish or variable, I didn't take time to realize that not only would it be impossible to please everyone all the time, but it wasn't worth attempting.

In reality, you can plan for the max, or you can plan for the average, but you can't do both.

It's like when I was growing up, and our church's attendance tripled every Easter. There would be standing room only, remote parking, and not enough Bibles to go around. But that was OK, because on average Sundays there were plenty of seats, parking, and Bibles.

There are exceptions, of course, or at least nuance. Amazon or UPS *needs* to build their system to accommodate the holiday rush. That's a big part of their bread and butter—it's a reasonable expectation. Still, they build in the capacity to flex up and down, using temporary labor, flex facilities, and varying schedules. They don't let the maximum need determine the main offering across the board.

But for most of us, the lesson is simple. Don't build the church for Easter. ■

EVERYBODY WANTS TO GO TO HEAVEN, BUT NOBODY WANTS TO DIE

"**B**randon" was an exceptionally talented candidate. Sharp, friendly, focused, and motivated, he was that rare "no-brainer" hire. Throughout my interview with him, I found myself daydreaming about his bright future with us: I couldn't wait to make him an offer.

What really clinched it for me was a comment he made at the end: "What I love most about this place is your commitment to training and development. I want to work my way up, and I'll be glad to know that the company has my back, because I'm in it for the long haul."

As it turned out, the expression "long haul" must have meant different things to the two of us. Brandon quit four months later because he "simply couldn't afford to wait any longer." Apparently he'd been offered another opportunity that paid more money. I assumed it must be a lot more, since he was leaving so suddenly and seemed sure it was the best move for his future and his family. But it only turned out to be about $300 more a month after taxes.

This was a short-sighted move. At his six-month anniversary with us, Brandon would have gotten a similar raise, and after a year his compensation would have nearly doubled. Plus, the new job required him to work many more hours than he had with us, including more weekends.

If Brandon had just done what he said he wanted to do—sit still, learn his craft, and grow with our company— he could have had everything he wanted. It was just a matter of time. The only advantage of the other job was that it promised rewards *today*.

When I heard from him again a year later, he was on his third job since leaving our company, making scarcely more than he had when he started with us, and working longer hours. Which meant even more time away from the family he wanted to provide for.

I understand that people want to move up and earn what they're worth, and that talented people have lots of opportunities. But being patient and building a solid foundation still plays a role that's too easily forgotten. If something is worth having, it's worth grinding for and waiting for. If you don't sacrifice for what you want, what you want will end up *being* the sacrifice. ■

EXCUSES DON'T EXPLAIN, EXPLANATIONS DON'T EXCUSE

Will is one of my very dear friends. The type that you're glad to have on your team, because you'd never want to look up and see him on the other side.

He's had an extraordinarily successful career and is certainly smart, talented, and capable. But if I were to attribute his success to a single factor, it would be his discipline. Will is a man of his word: If he says he's going to do something, he does it. And if you work with or around him, he'll expect the same of you.

Holding that type of high standard isn't about being inflexible or Draconian. Of course we all understand that "life happens." But when you hold yourself to a high standard of accountability and expect the same of others, the resulting mutual accountability builds trust—and that's when the magic can happen.

Will's mantra, his credo, his self-governing principle is that excuses don't explain, and explanations don't excuse. Now, I'm not saying there aren't sometimes legitimate reasons why we can't deliver on our commitments. I'm just saying no one wants to hear them. ■

Under normal circumstances Chewy was down to eat anything at any time, but she knew a setup when she saw one.

FEATURES TELL,
BENEFITS SELL

The top-10 best-selling infomercial products have earned nearly $10 billion in combined revenue. One of the main reasons for their success is that infomercial marketers are great at selling benefits, rather than just touting features.

Proactive didn't sell salicylic acid solution with benzoyl peroxide, they sold effortlessly clear skin and the confidence that came with it.

George Foreman didn't sell lightweight, electric-plate grills with removable fat drip pans. He sold convenient meal prep and the opportunity to eat healthier.

P90X didn't sell a 16-DVD set with total-body workout sessions and a meal guide, they sold ... well, beach bodies. About five million of them.

People don't buy features, specs, or product descriptions. They buy the benefits that come from having those things. There's a big difference between explaining what a product can do, and explaining what it can do *for me*. If you can't answer the second question, don't start pitching until you can. ■

INSIGHTS

FIRST SHARPEN YOUR AXE, THEN CUT THE TREE

All too often, when tasked with solving a problem, we just start "spitballing"—firing out ideas haphazardly until something "sticks"—in hopes that once we hit the mark we can all nod, agree, and move on to the next thing. That may work on TV, but in real life it's far more effective to spend the early part of any problem-solving session framing and defining the challenge itself.

- *What are we trying to solve?*

- *What would success look like?*

- *What have we tried before?*

- *What can we learn from what we've tried?*

- *Why haven't previous attempts to solve this been successful?*

- *How would we know if we'd found something better?*

I ask questions like these, and many, many others, to sharpen my problem-solving axe, so that when I finally take it to the "trunk" of the problem, I'm much more likely to fell the tree.

As a wise person once said, "If you gave me an hour to solve the world's problems, I'd spend the first 55 minutes defining what the problem is." That's easier said than done, I can assure you. But if you can find the discipline to pull it off, the results are well worth it. ■

INSIGHTS

IF IT'S KNOWABLE, MAKE IT KNOWN

I recently ran across an original 1990 World Book Encyclopedia collection. Even if you're old enough to remember using encyclopedias yourself, it's still hard to really recall a time before virtually any question could be answered in seconds, without even getting up from your chair.

Back then, a term paper could take days or even weeks, and might include trips to several libraries, bookstores, or even universities to find the information you needed. And the burden of proof was still very high: People checked your citations and reviewed your sources. The oft-quoted expression "trust but verify" was the rule of the day, and people operated accordingly.

So it's particularly odd to realize that now, when knowledge is cheaper than ever, we seem less willing to pay the cost of acquiring it. We take sources at face value rather than reviewing them ourselves. We make assumptions rather than doing our research. And we're comfortable answering "I have no idea" when we could have, not just some idea, but a fairly well-informed one, in no time flat.

Making the knowable known isn't just about doing more research, though—it's also about anticipating questions when you present your ideas to others. When information is cheap, choosing not to get it makes you look lazy. Better to think ahead and get informed. ∎

HAPPINESS WON'T MAKE YOU GRATEFUL, BUT GRATEFULNESS WILL MAKE YOU HAPPY

My wife Nimisha and I were finishing breakfast, watching a beautiful sunrise bouncing off Makana Mountain on our last day of vacation. Suddenly the ding of a text message disrupted our peace. This was odd—I'd turned off notifications. I glanced down:

EMERGENCY ALERT—BALLISTIC MISSILE THREAT INBOUND TO HAWAII. SEEK IMMEDIATE SHELTER. THIS IS NOT A DRILL.

The hotel dining room erupted in hysterics. Some people looked for shelter, others for provisions. Many gathered in prayer circles, praying for mercy, or for protection, or for peace. Others opted to enjoy their last meal as they waited for the end. Most people will never know how they'd react to staring down death, but we do. My wife and I declared our love for each other and phoned our immediate family to say goodbye.

Then, just as suddenly, the crisis was over. The message had been a mistake. There was no missile. I've never exhaled so hard in my life and I don't think anyone else there had either.

Over Mai Tais that afternoon, we reflected on our scare, and a predictable question came up: When you thought you were going to die, did you have any regrets about your life?

At first, I said no. But the more I thought about it, the more I realized I did have one important regret. I realized that the reason I had no big personal or professional regrets was because of amazing people throughout my life. I was incredibly fortunate. But even though I appreciated them, I hadn't shared it as much as I could have. If I'd died on the island that day, my "secret" would have died with me.

That made me sad. I wanted to thank the relatives who'd supported and cared for me, the teachers and professors who encouraged me, the mentors and advisors who invested time in my development, the friends who had my back and heard me during tough times, the partners who invited me to work alongside them, the teammates who joined us in the trenches, the investors who trusted us, the communities that embraced my business and my family.

Today, this is no longer an idea—it's become my way of life. I express my gratitude often, and as I do, it makes me happier and happier. In fact, studies show that where gratitude abides, depression, envy, and sadness cannot. Of course, it's a journey, and I'll still gripe about long lines at the grocery or slow wifi on a plane.

But, since that day, I realize that not only is the life that I have a tremendous blessing, but the fact that I get to continue living it is too. ∎

"The heat of the flames on my feet makes me feel thankful my feet aren't on fire."

INSIGHTS

IF YOU CAN'T BUY IT TWICE, YOU CAN'T AFFORD IT

J ulie was what retail salespeople call a "payment shopper." She desperately needed a car, but she didn't particularly care what make, model, or style. In fact, the only thing she seemed to care about was keeping her payments under $500 per month.

While that sounds like a simple request, experienced sellers and buyers know that many roads can get you there. Is your credit good? Are you putting money down? Are you willing to finance for a longer term? The answers to these questions and others can completely change the definition of a good outcome.

In Julie's case, she'd been living in her sister's basement with her two daughters for four years while she saved up about $9,000 for a down payment. Given her situation, I thought Julie would be pleased to know we could easily keep her payments below $500 without even using her entire savings for a down payment. She'd have enough to maybe get her own place, invest a little, do something nice for her kids.

Instead, she made the same unfortunate choice that a lot of buyers make: figure out the most they can "afford," based on some arbitrary percentage of income or debt-to-income ratio (or just their willingness to spend), and then push it to the limit.

Julie reasoned that she was making good money now, her expenses were low, and it would be best to get a "nicer" car (read: more expensive). So, she put the $9,000 down on a $28,000 vehicle, and financed the balance for seven years at 18 percent interest. Having maxed out her budget, she declined to pay for a warranty.

Just to make this absolutely clear, "rainy day" funds are for emergencies, not "making it rain."

The payment came in well under $500, which was what she wanted, but by the time she'd paid off the already five-year-old vehicle, she would have paid half its original value just in interest. In fact, she'd pay more in interest alone than the total cost of the other car we could have sold her.

Adding insult to injury, because she'd completely depleted her cash savings plus taken on large new monthly expenses, she couldn't afford to take care of the vehicle and deferred a good deal of important maintenance. Eventually, the car began to fail.

She had no choice but to either continue making payments on a broken-down vehicle or voluntarily surrender it, ruining her credit. Ultimately, her car was repossessed. She lost all the money she'd put into it and had to go back to her sister's basement with no car, no cash, and no credit.

The good news is that "Julie" isn't real. The bad news is that she's a composite of dozens of people I've encountered with similar stories or worse. Whether it's a car, a home, a vacation, or even a business, going all the way to the red line is a risky move.

Sure, risk is part of life and sometimes you have to reach the edge of the branch to get the fruit, but don't put yourself in a situation you can't recover from. Generally speaking, if you can't buy it twice, you can't afford it. ■

IF YOU WANT TO KNOW WHAT SOMEONE WANTS, LOOK AT WHAT THEY HAVE

nterviewing is an imperfect science. The interviewer is trained to find and expose fault, while the interviewee is trained to hide any and all imperfections. Combine that with the fact that most interviews only last 15 to 30 minutes, and you can see why it's basically a coin flip.

Similarly, because interviewees are so focused on projecting a positive image, they often miss the interviewer's red flags entirely, basically taking the company's website and job description at face value.

I've been on both sides of the process and in many different contexts. I've been a job candidate and a hiring manager; I've raised money from investors and invested my own; I've been a contestant and a judge. In all that experience, I've consistently seen that the key to understanding what the other

My biggest strength? Prolly my professionalism.
I keep it profesh AF namsayin?

party wants, I mean what they *really* value, is understanding what they already have.

This goes beyond simple behavioral interviewing techniques; this is about empathy and observation. The more you can put yourself in someone else's shoes and, more importantly, think in their terms, the better you'll understand what they want and value.

The reality is, I've learned more about this principle from all the times I missed its power than from the times I recognized it. How many times have I offered more money to convince someone to stay, when they told me they valued more balance—or pitched the value of work/life balance to people who just wanted more money? How many times have I touted boosts in profits or sales to people who cared about the mission and values—and talked about the mission and values to people who only cared about the bottom line?

People can and do change, but past behavior and values are still an incredibly powerful predictor; too powerful to be ignored.

As Maya Angelou said, when someone shows you who they are, believe them. Even better, don't wait for them to "show you," but learn how to see it for yourself. ■

INSIGHTS

NEVER OUTRUN YOUR HEADLIGHTS

Riding a motorcycle on an open highway is, in my opinion, one of the most thrilling experiences a person can have. However, riding at night is altogether different, as the added risks from low visibility and inattentive drivers makes the experience more stressful than "free."

It should be obvious that lower visibility makes it more difficult to see, but it may be less obvious that it also makes it hard to gauge your speed and the speed of others, as well as to react to obstacles and traffic. Also, the lighting system on the average bike really only provides a few feet of visibility under the best conditions, so on a dark night without much street lighting, you're really pressing your luck.

This is precisely why one of the golden rules of motorcycle riding is to never outrun your headlights. The rule doesn't depend on your experience level, the quality of your bike, or your risk tolerance. It's hard and fast. Because, no matter who you are, what you can't see *can* hurt you.

In business and in life, the analogy may be taking on more responsibility than you can effectively handle, or working on projects that are beyond your current skill level, or simply not allowing yourself space to handle the many demands on your attention. In those cases (and many others), it's not always best to press ahead at full speed. Sometimes the better choice is to accept that certain conditions require us to slow down, regain control, and stay the course until we find a little more daylight.

When you feel that pressure to push ahead at top speed, remember that slowing down to avoid a wreck is better than stepping on the gas and making one more likely. As Confucuis said: "It does not matter how slowly you go, as long as you do not stop." ∎

Even on a closed-course, Earl never took chances when it came to safety.

INSIGHTS

PEOPLE DON'T NEED TO BE TOLD, THEY NEED TO BE REMINDED

Atypical day with my three-year-old daughter, Diya, will inevitably include uttering any (or all) of a litany of phrases a couple dozen times:

Remember to share! Are you being kind? Say "excuse me" when Mommy and Daddy are talking. Ask nicely if you want something. Use your words. Cough in your elbow. Are you sure you don't have to go potty?

Diya is very bright and certainly strong-willed, but not obstinate by any means. In fact, she really tries her hardest to comply with what we teach her, and you can see almost daily improvement. But that improvement doesn't come from a single interaction, or even a few of them. It's the cumulative

effect of consistent feedback, routines, and the faith that she'll eventually "get it."

With a toddler, that seems intuitive. We can easily accept that no one comes out of the box primed and ready to be a kind, considerate, and productive human being. But with adults, we figure they should be finished products, or at most one-and-done when it comes to instruction and development.

The truth is, though, that even when we master something, a key tenet of continuous improvement is regularly revisiting the basics, refining our technique, and remembering (or being reminded of) core principles.

In many cases, people already "know" what they need to know, they just need to be reminded—constantly and perpetually. A big part of being an effective leader is not only being up for that challenge, but being wholly committed to it. ∎

INSIGHTS

THE HERD MOVES AT THE SPEED OF THE SLOWEST BUFFALO

An early mentor of mine once told me that the "speed of the captain determined the speed of the boat." The saying resonated with me, because it helped set the tone for my style and level of involvement. It also reminded me that I was accountable for my department's results and that the team could only work as well as I led them.

However, while this is directionally true, in reality any system is limited by the capacity of its bottlenecks—and teams, departments, or even companies are no exception to that rule.

In nature, systems regulate themselves. Slow buffalos get killed off, and the herd of remaining buffalos evolves to move faster in their absence. Lots of modern organizations follow a similar protocol (well, not literally) by culling the bottom 10 to 20 percent of performers each year, through bottom grading or "up or out" programs. But there is another way.

Unlike wild animals, people have an opportunity to train and develop our slower "buffalos" to help them get faster. We can also build cultures and environments to support the notion that no matter how fast we go or how high we climb individually, as a body we can only move as fast as the slowest among us.

The winner-take-all, dog-eat-dog drama is good for reality TV and game shows, but real life is more collaborative, by necessity. We win more when more of us win. In the long run, organizations that have figured out ways to make slower "buffalos" run faster will win out over those that just let them get killed off. Sure, occasional pruning is necessary to ensure the overall health and functioning of an organization, but it should be the exception and not the rule. ■

INSIGHTS

KEEP YOUR
GUARD UP

During a recent trip to India, I got to participate in one of the most striking and unique cultural experiences that lovely country has to offer—the bazaar.

As a retail entrepreneur, I love to study different approaches to sales and customer service. The Indian bazaar is particularly interesting, because it's about as different from modern western retailing as it gets. It's bigger, louder, faster, and more in-your-face than even the most bustling U.S. retail outlet on Black Friday. A true "see-it-to-believe-it" experience.

The vendors are extremely sharp, with keen instincts, and a home-court advantage that they use rather effectively. They've learned through experience how to turn seemingly benign questions like "What is your name?" and "Where are you from?" into profitable sales.

Ashok, a shop owner at a market outside of Jaipur, was truly one of the best I'd encountered. He was not only a gifted linguist—he spoke five languages fluently—but also a master at building rapport, a skilled negotiator, and a veritable human calculator. I was excited for the challenge of haggling with him, but still could scarcely overcome the feeling that I was wearing pajamas to a black-tie event.

I was eyeing a t-shirt rather excitedly, which practically invited Ashok's sales pitch. After some pleasantries, his opening offer of 1,200 rupees ($18) was miles from my paltry 200-rupee ($3) bid and frankly surprised me. I thought I was being fair, but his obviously feigned shock still somehow made me feel stingy. We went back and forth—he offered two for X and three for Y to sweeten the deal.

After several rounds of this, I could no longer keep up well enough to know if the offers even made sense. There may have even been a time or two when I countered against myself! When the dust finally settled after 10 minutes or so, I handed Ashok a 500-rupee note ($7.50). Despite the fact that I was "robbing him," he agreed to honor the deal because the shirt "looked good on me." A sucker for a compliment, I knew then that had he said that sooner, there's a good chance he'd have made even more money in less time.

When I returned to my hotel that evening, I happened to pass the gift shop again, and there, hanging in the window in plain sight, was the exact shirt I'd just "stolen" from Ashok … on sale for 200 rupees! And, as I knew all too well from my own negotiations earlier, that was just the starting ask.

This was humbling. Here I thought I was this hotshot salesman and negotiator, but I'd been pegged for a rube and taken for a ride. But once I got past my ego, I realized that was the best seven and a half bucks I'd ever spent. It was cheap tuition for a valuable lesson: that, no matter what you do and how well you do it, it only takes one punch to get knocked out. ∎

"That Rolex you sold me was a fake."

THE ONLY CONSTANT IS CHANGE

Business schools used to teach that companies had four levels of growth: start up, grow, mature, and decline. These days, however, with the advances in technology and market dynamics in general, that model no longer holds. The new one? Start up and grow. That's it, because the second you stop growing, you're already declining.

I've been fortunate to join and build companies that embraced this mindset, and I've met literally hundreds of candidates who wanted to work with us because they were so excited about rapid growth, massive responsibilities, new skills, and boatloads of cool experiences. However, about four months in, sometimes sooner, I'd notice that the newer folks would hit a dip, and some had trouble clawing their way through.

Our check-ins and informal meetings started to give us a clue what was going on. People were accustomed to joining

"CHANGE IS GOOD. BILLS ARE BETTER."

an organization and being uncomfortable for a bit, but then "settling in." After all, that had been their experience, whether with a new job, new school, or new neighborhood. You get there, spend a couple months figuring it out, and eventually you can coast for a bit.

But while that may be a typical process, growth-minded companies are anything but typical. We were in perpetual growth mode. Always growing, always changing.

Our new teammates wanted growth, excitement, and novelty, but they didn't know what it entailed. Constant growth means never being an expert, never being complacent, and rarely seeing the same thing twice. That's a stark contrast from the familiar comfort that comes from settling in.

In perpetual growth mode, the thing you get used to is the thing that's next up for the chopping block. Nothing is ever good enough, and there are no sacred cows, because they're slaughtered long before anyone can make them sacred.

Happiness in that world requires shifting your mindset from comfort-seeking to challenge-seeking and growth- seeking. Ironically, seeking new challenges actually broadens your comfort zone, so in the end you'll actually have more of what the comfort-seekers crave—and you'll be able to find it in many more places. ■

INSIGHTS

IF YOU THINK LONG, YOU THINK WRONG

Accepting "hold deposits" is a time-honored tradition in car sales.

In traditional dealerships, dealers may accept a nominal deposit, usually refundable but occasionally not, as security for a particular vehicle. This gives buyers some additional time to make up their minds or arrange financing, and it's often used to push undecided buyers further along in the sales process.

But we wanted our dealership to be anything but traditional. And we didn't accept hold deposits.

Instead, we opted for a policy that was radically different, and perhaps even shocking to most buyers: We did not hold vehicles under any circumstances. First come, first served.

"Just shoot! You're thinking about it too much!!"

We weren't trying to play a game or manipulate people into making decisions prematurely, we were just trying to remove ourselves completely from their decision-making process. Essentially, we were saying: *When you're ready, you can buy a car. If you're not, you can't.* Airlines run out of tickets, hotels run out of rooms, and dealerships sell out of cars.

When that happens, it's not their fault. Not everything works out with your timing, and that's OK. It's only tragic if you actually *did* make a decision but were simply afraid to act—the classic case of "if you think long, you think wrong."

We saw it all the time. *I love the car, I love the price, I love your team ... just let me go home and think about it.* But the next day, someone else who had done that homework ahead of time realized the same opportunity and seized it. The brutal fact was that we didn't sell the car out from under those customers—they let it go.

We might wish we had another one to sell them, but we didn't. We could offer them this lesson for free, though: When you're looking for an opportunity, know enough in advance to recognize the right one when it comes along. Once you make your decision, own it. And if you can't make your decision in time, at least own that you didn't. ■

INSIGHTS

WEAR YOUR BELT AND SUSPENDERS

S end an email AND leave a voicemail. Set an alarm AND request a wake-up call. Turn on auto-save AND backup your files.

Put it on your calendar AND set a reminder.

There's never any harm in wearing your belt and your suspenders too. It's better to leave no chance of being caught with your pants down. ∎

"Really?"

EVERYTHING THAT HAPPENS TO YOU ISN'T ABOUT YOU

After a hectic, but wonderful, weekend in Manhattan, my family and I waited at Newark airport for an early evening flight back to Richmond. My wife, Nimisha, and I had gotten to spend a little adult time with friends, while our two-year-old, Diya, spent time with grandparents.

Nimisha and I were happily telling stories of our weekend. Not to be outdone, Diya regaled us with tales of "Nani and Dada" spoiling her as only grandparents can—with trips to the park, bowls of ice cream, and even an introduction to Mr. Chuck E. Cheese!

We were all in high spirits, but also eager to get home. Moments before our scheduled boarding time, Diya asked if she could use the potty. Impressed with her "big girl" decision, Mommy eagerly complied, and they went to the restroom hand-in-hand, with smiles on their faces.

As I basked in good spirits and pride in my perfect little family, a loud shriek broke through the ambient noise of the hurried travelers. Some kid was having a tantrum. As a relatively new parent, I've been there myself, and my heart went out to the poor parents who had to deal with that situation. But I admit I also felt grateful and maybe even a tad superior that it wasn't us; our daughter was in such great spirits.

Then, as I heard the shriek a second time, and a third, and the voice got closer and louder, I realized that those poor parents *were* us. These terrible shrieks that seemed to echo and reverberate through every corner of EWR's tiny, cramped, and severely outdated Terminal A came from that little mouth that had been beaming moments before. And they only stopped when Diya took a breath, each successive scream louder than the prior as they came from deeper and deeper within her soul.

Around us, the glares and eye rolls began. Now, I've dealt with meltdowns before. Every parent has. But I usually have an out. At home, I have more levers to deal with the situation. At a store or restaurant, I can simply leave (with Diya in tow, of course). But here at the airport, trapped just beyond the security gate, and in open view of all those hostile, judging faces, it felt like an entirely different game.

Like any other toddler, Diya is a perfect angel, except when she's not. That's what you expect … she's a kid. But now it felt personal and humiliating; she was being unreasonable and she wasn't being fair to me or my wife. How dare she do this to us? And after such a great weekend, no less?

I went on in my head like this for some time before I caught myself, realizing that I was turning my daughter's discomfort around and making it about *me*. Rather than focusing all my attention on what my daughter needed, I was focused on the stares and the judgment of people that I didn't even know, let alone care about the way I do my daughter.

Every eye roll, scoff, and disgusted "here we go again" face dug at my ego. My need to appear competent and in control was threatened, and I didn't like it one bit.

Once this realization hit, I was able to understand that it was actually reasonable that Diya might have a meltdown after several very action-packed days away from home. The fairy-tale ending would be for me to tell you that the moment that I realized this error, I tuned into Diya's needs and was able to calm her effectively. But this ain't a fairytale, and her ex-hausted, overstimulated outburst didn't magically evaporate.

What *did* happen, though, was just as magical. The very moment I realized my error, I stopped giving a damn what anyone else thought. And, as I stopped keeping track of the dirty looks, I found that the real problem—my ego and not Diya's crying—was solved.

Ironically, I'd been a guest not long before on a podcast about living one's values, when I'd shared some lessons I thought I'd learned on this very point. Through my life's experiences, I'd learned long ago not to pin my happiness on others' approval. But Diya took it to another level. She showed me that while I wasn't an approval seeker, disapproval still stung. And my sense is that the happiest and most successful among us have developed an immunity to both approval and disapproval.

Thank you, Diya. Watching you grow up is helping me grow up, too. I appreciate the many lessons you've given me and the ones we have yet to share. ■

Completely out of quarters, Dave did what he had to do to quell Ryan's tantrum.

WHAT GOT YOU HERE MAY NOT GET YOU THERE

n most organizations, employees earn leadership roles by showing proficiency at the level just below. Good salespeople get promoted to sales managers, good teachers get promoted to principals, good lawyers become judges, and so on. The problem is that this approach, while sensible on its face, ignores a truth that's typically not recognized until someone has leveled up to the point they're no longer successful. That is the idea that "what got you *here* may not get you *there*."

A good salesperson may be a great closer, but a good manager needs to be a good listener, too. A great teacher may be a good instructor, but a principal needs to be good at organizing, too. And a good lawyer may be able to argue a case, but a good judge also needs to weigh the facts independently.

Career jumps like these, regardless of the field you're in, require a whole other set of skills that can be incredibly dif-

"I started out fetching."

ficult to learn on the job. Most newly promoted managers find this out the hard way, and compensate by doing more of what made them successful in the past, and doing it harder. But that's like slamming down the accelerator on a car that's out of gas: No matter how much you do it, you still lack the one thing that makes it go.

Acknowledging that what got you where you are isn't necessarily all it will take to get you where you want to go is by no means a hopeless admission of failure. It just means realizing that leveling up will require new skills and abilities. The people who are most successful in the long run recognize this and work hard to add to their skill set, so that they can always get from here to there, wherever "there" may be. ■

INSIGHTS

GOOD JUDGMENT COMES FROM EXPERIENCE, AND EXPERIENCE COMES FROM BAD JUDGMENT

If I were to boil this entire book down to a single idea, it would be this:

Good judgment comes from experience, and experience comes from bad judgment.

I reflect on this simple maxim almost daily. It's deceptively simple, yet remarkably powerful. We're often so hard on ourselves and others for making mistakes that we forget this truth: Mistakes are the way we learn to know better and, once we know better, we do better.

I didn't write this book because I think I have all the answers. In fact, I wrote it because I *know* that I don't. The point of me sharing this, and you reading it, is not for you to take my lessons as your lessons. Rather, I hope it will help you see life as your own series of lessons that you can collect and reflect on in your own way. Perhaps some of my lessons can become kernels of yours.

After all, good judgment comes from experience, and experience comes from bad judgment, but who says that the experience or the bad judgment have to be your own? If any of what I've shared here can help you avoid unnecessary pain or expense, it was worth my time to share it.

If you want to share some of your lessons or the ways you've adapted the lessons in this book, please email me at aaron@aaronmontgomery.com or text me at 804-496-1431. ∎